Oil

Lora Ala

BookLeaf
Publishing

India | USA | UK

Presentation by *BookLeaf Publishing*

Web: www.bookleafpub.com

E-mail: info@bookleafpub.com

ISBN: 9789357446792

First edition 2022

DEDICATION

To all the women

standing in kitchens

over baked banana cookies

solving life together.

bread

They had to be right
soft and flakey -
dense and filling.
Pan de Sal,
local.

Was 12 too many?
Any fewer could leave him wanting.
Did 12 indicate some overt eagerness?
There was a bag of 6.
But would 6 be too few?

(*Oh, it was the first one I picked up!*)
I'd lie.

(*I didn't even think about it*)
As though I were about to be interrogated.

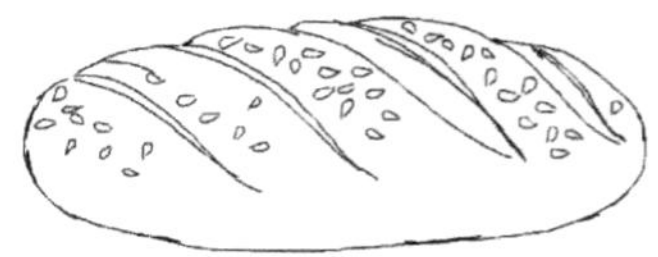

paused

I plated the meal.
Bread rolls in the centre.
Then off to the side.
Then askew.
(*I just threw them down!*)

Ready, waiting.

(*You've got great timing!*)
I'd lie.

(*I just finished getting it all ready.*)
As if I hadn't been paused in my kitchen,
A shell.
A chitinous near-humanoid.

(*Don't wait for me*)
He was blunt.

(*I won't.*)
I'd lie.

dance

The sound of a door is a terrifying
click, slide, swing.
A performance must begin immediately.

The curtain has been drawn,
The audience is seated,
The lights sear.

I lift one arm, reaching high,
fingers delicate,
wrists straight,
my right leg swinging back into a long
arabesque.

He enters to see the one plate I am holding,
ready to wash.
It's been ready to wash for 20 minutes,
but it wasn't time yet.

(*Great timing!*)
I'd lie. Jeté.

(*It's all just finished. Hungry?*)
He'd watch. Plié.

The audience stiffens. The next part must be just
right.
They know how difficult it will be.
How effortless an expert makes it look.
The first bite tastes of nothing, nothing, nothing.

Until,
(delicious)
he squawked.

The grande adage.

comfort

(*I started that book you recommended.*)
I'd pick at the remnants of conversation sitting
on my plate
I wouldn't say how I hated it.
How it was full of the sort of men I couldn't
stand.
Brusque, hardened, emotionless.
Surrounded by dead women with shiny white
faces.
Who kowtowed eagerly,
Begging for affection.

I'd put a morsel in my mouth to chew,
considering the silence with analytical fervor.
It shows our comfort. How natural we must be.
But I am uncomfortable.

Two slices were left.
I took the worse of the two and looked for
something recognizable in his expression.
(*It's wonderful.*)
I'd lie.

expertise

I can't remember how many meals
invented, stolen, dissected—
have been basted, broiled
steamed, seared.

Delicately managed
with attentive fingers
fearing any flaw.

(*It was easy*)
I'd lie.

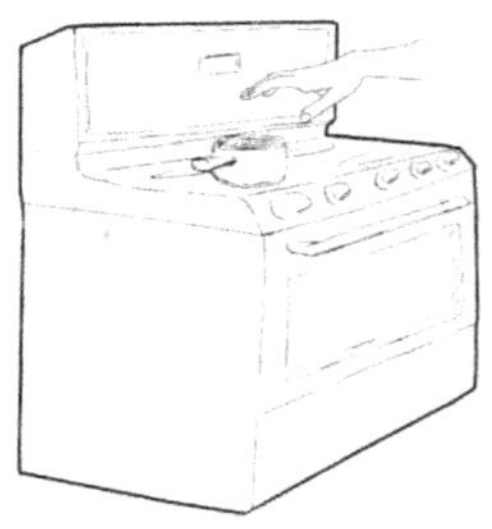

luggage

He ate six of them that night—a sign,
I wrongly thought,
of his feelings towards me.

I had eaten two,
and wanted a third.

It was less than a week later,
I had packed up a life,
rolled tee shirts,
a computer cord,
two dog-eared books,
a pitiful array of glosses and tinctures,
into a small canvas
and left.

I unpacked and packed,
ad nauseum.
Each time hopeful of a new affirmation
pieced together from shards of my resolve.

sway

I found comfort in a rocking chair.
swinging back and forth,
with a momentum that might tip forward,
and spill me out
across the ground,
to melt and seep
into the floorboards.

Each crescendoed moment
precariously placed
upon a precipice—
a sudden return.
Leaping backwards now,
held back from an edge
that I willed myself over.

oil

I want to be like the oil
I dip my bread into,
and spread on pans,
and broccoli,
and meat.

Smooth,
coating lovingly,
and bettering each bite.

But I am like oil,
sticky and burning.
oversaturating and
burdening
without relent.

write

I kept a record:
a book of burning moments
salted words
and peppered actions.

At one point I'd open it and scrawl,
pressing letters like a poultice
to seep into the page,
mucking the rot.

I had another too:
A cookbook. A collection.
Recipes that mitigated disasters
and replicated a tenderness bereft.

I don't make them anymore.
I don't write those words, either.

photo

I held, for a moment, a picture of us.
It was fabricated from fantasies
of foreign travels
and unforgettable feasts.

When it was twisting and folding
inwards on itself from the heat
of a flame held too close,
I'd imagine the softness
of the light scattered on your face,
and the joy
of the warmth enveloping us at last.

I have that now,
with another.
It's a memory,
not some folly
for the naive.

banquet

How many carcasses of
chickens,
cows,
pigs,
turkeys,
groves of fruit trees,
leaves,
mined minerals,
and foraged herbs
plated themselves akimbo,
dressed in their finest sweets and sauces,
and presented themselves
delightfully
to You.

reprieve

In my nadir,
when I was most enfeebled,
I stepped into the house of a friend
and let myself be loved
and attended to,
affectionately.

She held my hand
and moved it across the page
of your textured imperfections.
I felt then
my own self
carving deep crevasses,
measuring topographical impurities,
and razing them.

She stayed my hand,
and willed me to watch
as she deciphered them.
Runes from a tome
now turned legible.
You'd lied.

I watched as you alighted now,
luggage in tow,
from a freight in my mind.

again

On the first day,
I crawled
like an infant finding themself
unfettered.

But when I began to stand again
I realized my feet remembered the path,
I'd trodden before.
My fingers remembered how to turn and chop,
dice and season,
and bring warmth to a meal again.
My tongue remembered how to taste and feel
and enjoy what once was sand and glass.

I lit a small candle,
and kept vigil
over it.

When it went out,
I lit it again.

Again.

Again.

Again.

another

The first man
I dared to know again
after you
was all I needed
to know.

(*Why?*)
Because it didn't matter,
how many,
how much.
There was never going to be enough of me
for you.

I knew that then, when I felt the amount
that I had to give
when it was received,
with desire.

I realized how terribly stupid I had been
to think you could ever be more than you are.

For that, I'm sorry.
I had thought you so much more.
The fault is my own.

hunger

I devoured books,
hungry for some answer
that might explain
your callous kisses,
your cruel caresses.

I fell short
of the task.

I began to devour myself instead.
Thin sashimi slices of throat,
dashed with paprika
to accompany a stew,
a kidney or two,
a lung for good measure.

Braised chops of inner thigh,
a salad, delectable with shaved skin.

Plump breasts for dessert,
sugar sprinkled atop,
in that bowl
with the yellow flowers.

I gorged
until I was full.

words

I scrolled back
to the times
when we used to say words like
I love you
I miss you
I want you near me

and I counted:
how many of mine outnumbered yours?

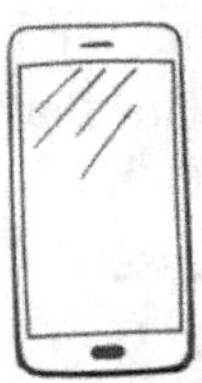

renew

I cannot wear
that blue-striped shirt,
or watch that climactic moment,
or drink that soft white,
and enjoy it anymore.

But I can
walk in new shoes,
read her poignant poems,
imbibe on blends and herbs,
and live anew.

burden

I took a right, a left, then another.
I stopped where we would once embrace.
Could our tire tracks still be seen?
Does the sun remember
how it would ache on our heads?
Does this wind recall my form?
What plains of tall grasses
could speak about us?
Have these pines wintered the needles
that pierced our soft skin?
Concrete pillars and asphalt ground
have silenced the footprints we gifted then.
And the birds that fly don't entreat me
with a visit and chirp of remembered times.

I hold the memories alone now.
I wear some and cannot scrub them away
With any salt, sugar, or stone.
I wear them.

run

On the first day,
I ran,
with a pride I had missed for too long
and a reciprocation that left me
whole.

I kept each foot moving,
and turned back once
only to see if the chase continued.

When it didn't,
I stopped and caught my breath,
relieved.

whole

When I finally closed the book,
and threw away your recipes,
and painted my walls
with the colour of my blood,
and furnished my home
with the bones of my body,
and cooked a meal made of my heart,
and walked in shoes built by my hands,
and held myself with the strength of my own
arms,

and
and
and

When I finally.

enjoy

I am surrounded
by the truth of myself
at the close
of this chapter.

I have overturned
all our lies,
and picked apart
the narrative
that I held too close
for too long.

It is finished
with me
and leaves me now
with the leftovers.

So I pick up a ladle,
and stir
and chop
and plate.

I season chicken thighs,
and stir asparagus,
and soak rice,

and feed myself
again.

and I am like the oil, once more.